Listening to Crickets

Listening to Crickets

A Story about Rachel Carson

by Candice F. Ransom
illustrations by Shelly O. Haas

A Carolrhoda Creative Minds Book

Carolrhoda Books, Inc./Minneapolis

For Ryan

Library of Congress Cataloging-in-Publication Data

Ransom, Candice F.
   Listening to crickets : a story about Rachel Carson / by
Candice F. Ransom ; illustrations by Shelly O. Haas.
      p.   cm. — (A Carolrhoda creative minds book)
   Includes bibliographical references (p.   ).
   Summary: Examines the life of the marine biologist and science
writer whose book "Silent Spring" changed the way we look at pesticides.
   ISBN 0-87614-727-9
   1. Carson, Rachel, 1907-1964—Juvenile literature. 2. Women
conservationists—United States—Biography—Juvenile literature.
3. Conservationists—United States—Biography—Juvenile literature.
4. Biologists—United States—Biography—Juvenile literature.
[1. Carson, Rachel, 1907-1964. 2. Environmentalists.
3. Biologists. 4. Science writers.] I. Haas, Shelly O., ill.
II. Title. III. Series.
QH31.C33R36 1992
574'.092—dc20
[B]   92-3470
                                                         CIP
                                                          AC

Manufactured in the United States of America

1 2 3 4 5 6 98 97 96 95 94 93

Table of Contents

① Summer Nights

Rachel stood very still. If she didn't move, not even a finger, she could almost become a part of the field she was standing in. If she was very quiet, the meadow—a busy world of insects and tiny animals working in the grass—would reveal its secrets to her. Maybe a bird would mistake her for a tree and land on her shoulder.

Suddenly Rachel's mother called her for supper. Her mother's voice carried from the house, through the apple orchard, to the field.

Rachel didn't move. Even though she heard her mother calling, she could hear other things, too. There was the whisper of the tall grass and knotweed she stood knee-deep in; the twitterings of sparrows settling down for the evening; the laughing cry of a robin as it flew off a fence post. She could even hear the tiny rustlings of small creatures—field mice and shrews—running along tunnels in the grass.

Rachel often roamed the woods and fields that surrounded her home. She had plenty of land to explore. In 1900, before Rachel was born, her father had bought sixty-five acres of land in Springdale, Pennsylvania, eighteen miles from Pittsburgh. Robert Warden Carson had hoped to develop the land, but he was too mild-mannered to be a successful businessman. Mr. Carson sold real estate and insurance while waiting for the right time to sell his land.

Now, seventeen years later, the Carsons still lived in Springdale. Although the Carson property was not a real farm, there were plenty of cows and chickens and pigs for Rachel to observe.

Sometimes Rachel rambled the countryside with her friends Irene Mills and Charlotte Fisher. But most of the time, Rachel was alone, except for her dog, Candy. Rachel was used to being alone. Her brother, Robert, was eighteen and her sister, Marian, was even older, twenty. They had busy grown-up lives that left little time for a ten-year-old sister tagging along.

Supper was a quiet affair that summer. Rachel's brother had gone to Texas to train in the U.S. Army Aviation Service. The United States had been involved in a war since the spring of that year, 1917. News of the fighting in Europe was splashed across the newspaper Mr. Carson read every evening.

Rachel knew her mother didn't want Robert to go overseas to fight against the Germans. But it was all so exciting! Rachel listened intently when her mother read Robert's letters aloud. One letter described the bravery of a Canadian pilot who had been shot down by a German pilot and survived. Rachel thought about that Canadian pilot again and again.

After supper Rachel would often curl up with the new issue of *St. Nicholas,* a popular magazine for children. She turned to the "St. Nicholas League" section, where there were stories and drawings by children. If the stories were very good, the writer could win a cash prize and an honor badge.

Rachel longed to be included in those hallowed pages. She had been writing stories and poems for years. Back in second grade, she'd made a "book" for her father, illustrated with her drawings of birds and animals. Her father still had it.

On these long evenings, Mrs. Carson would go over to the piano and run her fingers lightly over the keyboard. The Carson family usually sang together, but sometimes Mr. Carson would stand alone beside the piano. In his rich bass voice, he would sing the words to "Beautiful Ohio" and "Rocked in the Cradle of the Deep." Rachel loved songs and poems about the sea, even though she'd never glimpsed the ocean. Springdale, Pennsylvania, was a long way from the Atlantic shore. But she *would* see the ocean someday.

When the last notes died away, Mrs. Carson would remind Rachel it was time for bed. She made sure her youngest child got plenty of rest.

Once in bed, Rachel could hear the faint *plink, plink* of the piano as her mother resumed her playing. If Rachel did not feel like going to sleep right away, she would lean her arms on the windowsill and breathe in the fragrant night air.

Her keen eyes spied bats snatching insects on the wing. Rachel could tell the difference between bats and swallows—the swift birds wheeling in the purple sky above the barn, catching gnats.

From the darkness would come the familiar sound of crickets. Rachel listened to the *rachet, rachet* the unseen insects made by scraping their hind legs together. She often fell asleep to the crickets' song.

The September 1918 issue of *St. Nicholas* magazine felt heavy in Rachel's hands, and crisply new. She held her breath as she opened it to the "St. Nicholas League." Would it be there this time? Oh, let it be there.

It was!

Rachel couldn't believe her eyes, even though the proof was clearly printed in black and white. Her story! "A Battle in the Clouds" by Rachel L. Carson, age ten. And it had won the Silver Badge!

Rachel hadn't been able to forget the account of the brave Canadian fighter pilot. She had written a story about the pilot and mailed it off to *St. Nicholas* magazine. And now she was a published author.

Rachel knew her mother would be proud. Maria Carson had great respect for the written word.

She read aloud to her children nearly every evening, no matter how old they were. Rachel's earliest memories were of listening to her mother read *The Last of the Mohicans* or one of Charles Dickens's books. Rachel had listened with all her heart and soul, letting the rich prose wash over her like ocean waves. Maybe she would write stories, too! When she started school, Rachel learned to write, which gave her the tool she needed to put down on paper the stories she made up in her head.

Now, with her first success shimmering on the page before her, Rachel was sure she wanted to be a writer. She was even more certain when she received a check for ten whole dollars later that month. She was a published, *paid* author!

From that moment on, Rachel's pen fairly flew as she scribbled other stories. The war ended on November 11, 1918, and Robert came home safely. Rachel saw her name in print again. "A Message to the Front" was published in the February 1919 issue of *St. Nicholas* and earned her a Gold Badge. She became an Honor Member with "A Famous Sea-Fight," published in the August 1919 issue.

Rachel went on to high school, where she was an excellent student. Two days after her eighteenth birthday, Rachel graduated from Parnassus High School. This quiet, determined girl had important plans regarding the rest of her life. She was going to college to study literature. She was going to be a writer. *Nothing* would make her change her mind.

②

A Change of Course

The Pennsylvania College for Women suited Rachel's needs perfectly. It was a small school, with only about three hundred students. And it was close to home. More important, the school offered scholarships to students who needed financial assistance. Even with a scholarship, Rachel's college education was a struggle for the Carson family. Her father sold parcels of their land, but money was tight. The one hundred dollars the college awarded Rachel did not go far, even in 1925, the year she began school. Every penny from home went toward the cost of her tuition, room, and board.

Rachel was a serious student. She wasn't interested in going to the movies or to Reymar's soda fountain for a lime rickey. Many of the young women who attended the college were more interested in dances, dates, and parties than in their classes. Although Rachel was not unfriendly, she declined social invitations. She did not have the wardrobe for a full social life, and she did not want to waste her time trying to be popular.

Rachel could usually be found in her dorm room or at the library, studying. When she wasn't studying, Rachel was doing what she loved best— writing. The other girls envied Rachel's writing talent. She was a member of Omega, the literary club, and was on the staff of the college paper, the *Arrow*.

In her sophomore year, Rachel took her first biology class. She was still keenly focused on writing and literature, but students were required to take two semesters of science in order to graduate. Rachel's childhood curiosity about nature was reawakened. Her instructor, Mary Scott Skinker, made science exciting. Biology gave Rachel a whole new way to view the world. She began to observe nature again, not just with the eyes of a poet, but with the sharp, clear eyes of a scientist.

Rachel enrolled in a zoology class her junior year, even though her science requirement was fulfilled. On a field trip to McConnell's Mill, at the Cook State Forest, Rachel picked up a stone with the imprint of a fish skeleton on one side.

17

With wonder, she traced the outline of the fossil. She was touching evidence that proved fish once swam in deep waters on this very spot. Though she had yet to visit the sea, she felt its irresistible pull, much the way the moon tugs at the tides.

Then Rachel did the unthinkable. Halfway through her junior year, she boldly changed majors. She switched her course of study from literature to biology. It was as if her long-submerged love of nature suddenly pushed aside her goal to be a writer. She was going to be a scientist.

The other girls couldn't understand Rachel's decision. How could she give up literature, a worthy goal, for *science?* Mary Skinker warned Rachel that the road of a female scientist would be rocky. In the 1920s, science was not considered a "proper" career for a young woman. Rachel was aware that there were few jobs open to a female biologist. But she listened to her heart. She knew she was making the right move.

Changing majors so late in her course of study meant that Rachel had to catch up on the required science classes. She spent most of her senior year in the laboratory.

Despite her heavy course load, Rachel

graduated magna cum laude, with high honors, and was accepted as a scholarship student in the zoology graduate school program at Johns Hopkins University. But before starting graduate school, there was something important that Rachel had to do. She was on her way to meet her destiny—the sea.

An endless blue-gray line appeared on the horizon. Rachel could have drawn it with a pencil. Then she made out waves rolling onto the shore and seabirds arcing overhead.

Rachel Carson and the sea had met at last.

Rachel had arrived at the Woods Hole Marine Biological Laboratory on the coast of Massachusetts, where she would spend part of the summer.

The six weeks at Woods Hole sped by. Rachel worked in the laboratory, studying the nervous systems of snakes, lizards, and turtles. She and the other students also swam in the buoyant ocean, played tennis, and went to beach parties. Rachel didn't tan, but freckled in the strong summer sun. Never had work been so much fun.

More than anything, Rachel loved to be outdoors. Ocean breezes ruffled her bobbed hair as she observed squid, starfish, scallops—creatures she had only read about in books. She spotted crabs and anemones living in tide pools, rock-trapped pockets of water where sea life flourished. Rachel spent hours crouched in ankle-deep water, watching the activities of these fascinating creatures.

When summer was over, Rachel left for Baltimore to begin her graduate studies at Johns Hopkins University. After finding a place to live, she traveled to Washington, D.C., to visit the Bureau of Fisheries. Rachel knew she would need employment after she earned her master's degree.

She met with Elmer Higgins, who was chief of the bureau's biology division. Mr. Higgins was used to biology students inquiring about opportunities at the bureau. He told Rachel about the importance of marine biology and described the problems in the field of fishery research. Mr. Higgins also told Rachel what she had heard before, that there weren't many jobs open to female biologists, outside of teaching. Rachel was not discouraged. She knew she would be a scientist. But first she had to finish her education.

In October 1929, the stock market crashed, plunging the country into the Great Depression.

Stock prices plummeted. As a result, factories and businesses shut down. Many people were out of work, and life was grim.

Rachel missed her parents, who still lived in Pennsylvania. She found a small house to rent in Stemmer's Run, Maryland. It was only a few miles from her school yet close enough to the Chesapeake Bay to satisfy Rachel's craving to be near the sea. Then she began convincing her parents to leave Springdale and move to Maryland. Her parents were unwilling at first, but Rachel won them over with long-distance phone calls, telegrams, and special-delivery letters. In January of 1930, Rachel's parents moved from Pennsylvania into the house in Stemmer's Run. Rachel's brother, Robert, stayed in Pittsburgh, where he had a job.

Like most people during the Depression, the Carson family did not have enough money. Always resourceful, Rachel got a job as a teacher's assistant that summer. When the fall semester started, she found a part-time job as a laboratory assistant. Her life became a blur of classes all day and laboratory work at night.

In 1931, Robert's business in Philadelphia failed and he joined the family in Maryland. He landed a job in Baltimore as a radio repair estimator. As part payment on an estimate, he was given a white Persian cat named Mitzi, who became an important member of the Carson family. Both Mrs. Carson and Rachel loved cats. There had always been one or two of them around the house back in Springdale.

In June 1932, Rachel received her master of arts degree in marine zoology from Johns Hopkins University. She was a scientist. But where would she work?

Rachel continued to hold down two part-time jobs, one at the University of Maryland and the other at Johns Hopkins summer school. Her family scraped along until the summer of 1935. Then Rachel's father suddenly died.

At the age of twenty-eight, Rachel had to support herself and her mother. She needed a better job. She remembered Elmer Higgins, the man she had visited at the Bureau of Fisheries. She decided to call on him again.

As Rachel sat in Elmer Higgins's office, she was nervously aware that times were hard and jobs were scarce. The government wasn't about to hire just anyone, no matter how qualified.

Mr. Higgins told her the bureau was working on a series of radio broadcasts called "Romance

Under the Waters," which the staff jokingly called "Seven-Minute Fish Tales." Getting good scripts was a problem. He had a professional writer who knew nothing about marine biology and marine biologists who knew nothing about writing. He needed someone with knowledge of the subject who was also a good writer.

Mr. Higgins asked Rachel if she could write.

Rachel felt the first glimmer of hope. Could she write!

3

The Life of the Sea

It was only a temporary job. Rachel would work at home, writing radio scripts. And she would only be paid $19.25 per week. But Rachel was glad to have the job, any job, when so many walked the streets unemployed. When the radio project was over and Mr. Higgins didn't need her to write scripts anymore . . . well, she'd worry about that later.

She proved herself with her first script. Mr. Higgins read what she had written and immediately gave her another assignment. Rachel was delighted to combine her two favorite interests—science and writing.

Rachel and her mother fell into an agreeable routine. Mrs. Carson did the cooking and took care of the house. Rachel wrote scripts. Then their little family expanded without warning. Rachel's older sister, Marian, died. Marian's daughters, Virginia and Marjorie, who were both in grammar school, came to live with their aunt and grandmother.

The Carson family needed more room. They moved to a two-story house in Silver Spring, Maryland, a suburb near Washington, D.C. The rent here was higher than the place in Stemmer's Run, plus Rachel had two growing girls to feed and clothe. She needed a permanent job.

When Rachel learned of an opening at the bureau for a junior aquatic biologist, she decided to apply for the position. She was required to take an exam first. Rachel was the only woman to take the test, and she earned the highest score. The job was hers. Elmer Higgins wanted Rachel in his department. He valued her skills as both a writer and a scientist. Now Rachel was a permanent, full-time employee with a starting salary of two thousand dollars a year, twice what she had been earning as a part-time scriptwriter.

The Bureau of Fisheries decided to turn the "Fish Tales" radio scripts into a booklet. Rachel's writing style was both readable and graceful. She was the natural choice to rewrite the older radio material, which had been written by other people. Rachel turned the choppy scripts into smooth prose that was a joy to read.

When the "Fish Tales" booklet was finished, Mr. Higgins asked Rachel to write an introduction to link the articles together. Since the articles were about sea creatures, Rachel wrote about the environment that made their existence possible—the sea. She poured all she felt about the sea into the piece and proudly turned the essay in to her chief.

Elmer Higgins read her introduction, then told her it was not suitable. Not suitable! Rachel was stunned with disappointment. Did she not reveal the sea in all its glory and power? Wasn't this her best writing effort so far?

That was precisely the problem, Mr. Higgins informed her. Her writing was *too* beautiful; her descriptions of the sea were too poetic. The introduction overwhelmed the simple "Fish Tales" articles that followed. Mr. Higgins implied that what Rachel had written was too good for a government pamphlet and urged her to send her article to the *Atlantic Monthly,* a top-quality literary magazine.

Rachel put away the "Fish Tales" introduction. It *was* good, she felt, but not good enough for a prestigious magazine like the *Atlantic Monthly.*

But the experience of writing the "Fish

Tales" scripts and the booklet boosted Rachel's confidence. In the evenings and on weekends, whenever she could carve out the time, she wrote articles and sent them to the *Baltimore Sun* newspaper. "It'll be Shad-Time Soon—and Chesapeake Bay Fishermen Hope for Better Luck this Season" was the first of several articles published in the newspaper's Sunday magazine section. The *Sun* articles only brought in ten or fifteen dollars apiece, but Rachel was grateful for the much-needed money.

Even with a full-time job, and the bonus sales of newspaper articles, money did not stretch far in the Carson house. The Depression lingered, and times were hard for everyone. If only Rachel could make more money writing articles! Remembering her rejected "Fish Tales" introduction, Rachel dug it out and mailed it off to the *Atlantic Monthly,* as her boss had suggested months ago. The magazine could only say no, she realized. What did she have to lose?

Six weeks later, she received a check for seventy-five dollars. The *Atlantic* had bought her story! When "Undersea" appeared in the September 1937 issue, Rachel received an astonishing letter. Quincy Howe, an editor at Simon and Schuster publishing company, wrote asking Rachel if she'd ever thought of doing a book. Could she write a book? Rachel listened to her heart, as she'd once listened to crickets, and decided the life of the sea was worth knowing. She should tell that story.

Writing a book while holding down a full-time job was very difficult, she discovered. After her mother and nieces had settled down for the night, Rachel would go upstairs to the big bedroom and write page after page in longhand. Her only companions were her two Persian cats, Kito and Buzzie, who often drowsed on her notes.

Under the Sea-Wind was published in November 1941. Rachel was thirty-four years old. She proudly gave the first copy to her mother, who had typed Rachel's handwritten manuscript. The book was dedicated to her. The reviews were very good. No one had ever written a book about the sea from the point of view of the creatures who inhabited it. The reader learns about migration from a pair of shorebirds, and about the struggle for survival in the ocean from a baby mackerel.

Then the Japanese bombed Pearl Harbor, on December 7, 1941, and the world turned its attention to more important news. The United States was at war. Rachel's book was forgotten.

31

In 1940 the Bureau of Fisheries had become part of the newly formed Fish and Wildlife Service. Rachel's wartime assignment for the Fish and Wildlife Service was writing bulletins urging people to serve fish at meals. Meat was rationed on the home front in order to keep the fighting troops well supplied.

People relied too heavily on familiar types of fish like cod. Rachel's job was to introduce other types of fish and shellfish into American diets. Even though she advised millions of people to serve clams at the supper table, Rachel herself didn't like seafood!

At the end of the war, Rachel became chief editor for the information division of the Fish and Wildlife Service. She had a staff of six employees and an office with a large framed photograph of a Maryland blue crab as the only decoration. Her employees found her to be quiet and efficient. Her mind was keen, and she had a remarkable memory. She could quote paragraphs she'd dictated days before. Her work reflected her attention to detail. Rachel always double-checked her facts.

Yet Rachel had a humorous side. She dreamed up a prank that was the talk of the department for years. A fellow writer in the Chicago office wrote and published a sloppy bulletin about the cooking of wild game. Dismayed at the quality of the work, Rachel decided to play a trick on the woman.

Pretending to be a feature writer for an important national publication, Rachel composed a telegram. The telegram informed the Chicago woman the magazine would do a big story on her if she cooked *field mice* in mushroom sauce! Rachel was ready to send the message, until she found out it was against the law to send telegrams under a false name.

Although work kept her busy, Rachel was not satisfied. She had written one book about the sea. Now she wanted to write another. This book would be different. Instead of describing the creatures who lived in or near the sea, she would describe the sea itself. This would be a book that she often wished she could find in the library. It would be her most ambitious project yet.

Her second book proved to be much more difficult to write than her first book. Rachel was a slow, careful writer. She had little time to write, between her job and her duties at home. She worked best at night, and often went directly from her desk at home to her desk at the office. This schedule soon wore her down. But after six months with little sleep, Rachel had enough of a manuscript to show a publisher. She was successful. Oxford University Press sent Rachel a contract and gave her a deadline for the rest of the book.

Rachel knew she would not meet the deadline unless she was able to leave her job for a while. Yet she could not, because her family needed the money. Fortunately, help arrived. In August 1949, she was awarded a fellowship grant. The money from the grant allowed her to take an extended leave of absence from her government job.

Yet the time off proved to be very stressful. The Carson family moved to another house in Silver Spring, and for a while one of Rachel's nieces was ill. To make matters worse, when Rachel went back to her government job, she had to catch up on the work she had missed. In spite of everything, Rachel continued to work on her book throughout the fall of 1949 and the winter and spring of 1950, with her cat Tippy batting the typewriter keys.

At last the book was finished. It was scheduled to be published as *The Sea Around Us* in July

1951. Rachel was relieved the difficult task was over. She had written a book that made the reader experience the vastness and power of the sea. In her book, the sea was not just a rolling body of water, but an environment that worked with—and sometimes against—a more well-known environment: land. Rachel knew she had written a good book, but she had no clue what would happen next.

The Sea Around Us became an instant best-seller. At the age of forty-four, Rachel was famous. Her life would never be the same. As a best-selling author, she toured the country, autographing books and giving talks. Awards and honors poured in. She won the John Burroughs Medal for excellence in nature writing. She was the first woman to be given the Henry G. Bryant Medal of the Philadelphia Geographical Society. *The Sea Around Us* was the 1951 National Book Award winner for nonfiction.

But sudden fame had its downside, too. Rachel had always been a quiet, private person. Now she was pestered by people wherever she went. She was even badgered by a fan in the beauty parlor while her hair was in pin curls!

Success was exhausting. Rachel lost twenty

pounds from all the attention. She wanted to retreat by the sea and write. She had enough money, for once, so she resigned from her government job.

The future was calling her. It was time to listen.

4

Life on the Shore

The house rose from the rocks, almost part of the cliff that towered above Sheepscot Bay. Ever since Rachel had visited Maine years earlier, she'd longed for a house at the very edge of the sea. She and her mother had rented cottages in Maine during past summers, but now Rachel had a seaside cottage of her own.

With her earnings from *The Sea Around Us,* Rachel had bought a one-and-a-half-acre tract of land in West Southport, near Boothbay Harbor, Maine. The cottage she'd had built was simple, but the windows were large sheets of glass that let in vast views of sea and sky. With her bedroom only steps from the beach, Rachel had a laboratory literally at her feet.

The Carson family was much smaller by 1953. Rachel's nieces were grown, and Marjorie had a one-year-old son, Roger. Rachel, her mother, and her cat Muffin migrated north every spring, staying until October, when it was time to shut off the water pipes and return to Maryland.

The cottage was a wonderful place to relax. Mrs. Carson was crippled with arthritis, but her days were brightened by the loons and baby seals she glimpsed from the window. Once Rachel pointed out a whale splashing at the mouth of the harbor.

Revived by the salt air, Rachel was ready to get back to work. She had a new book contract. The Houghton Mifflin publishing firm had asked her to write a guidebook about shore life. Rachel was eager to start on the new book. Like most writers, she was always more interested in the work ahead of her than in what she had already accomplished.

With her biologist's belt loaded with specimen bottles and a magnifying glass, Rachel explored the tide pools near her cottage during low tide.

Rachel belonged here more than anyplace else in the world, shin-deep in chilly water, with the fog softly brushing her cheek, and the soothing *sush-sushing* of the water lapping against the rocks.

Research for the guidebook was endlessly fascinating and enjoyable, made even more so by the fact that Rachel had help. Bob Hines, an artist and longtime friend from the Fish and Wildlife Service, had been commissioned by Houghton Mifflin to draw the illustrations for Rachel's book. They worked together as a team, catching scurrying crabs for Bob to sketch or marveling at a colony of anemones clinging to the underside of a rock.

Rachel's editor, Paul Brooks, also visited the cottage. After supper, he and Rachel would peer through her microscope at creatures captured in Rachel's specimen bottles. They observed threadlike worms, tiny snails, and miniature sponges—inhabitants of an underwater fairyland. Then, no matter how late the hour, Rachel would carry the creatures in a bucket down the steep steps to the beach and return them to their home, the tide pools.

The Edge of the Sea was published in 1955. It

was much more than a guidebook. It described the life and geology of the East Coast, from the rocky shoreline north of Cape Cod, to the sandy beaches of the mid-Atlantic, to the coral reefs and mangrove coastline farther south.

The Edge of the Sea was nearly as successful as *The Sea Around Us*. Rachel was proud of her new book. It represented many happy hours sharing the world of the sea with friends and loved ones. This book also complemented her two earlier books. *Under the Sea-Wind* described life in and near the sea, and *The Sea Around Us* tackled the sea itself. Rachel wrote *The Edge of the Sea* with the word "ecology" uppermost in her mind. Ecology is the study of the way living things relate to their environment and to each other. Rachel did not simply want to catalog seashells, as one might find in a guidebook. She wanted people to know about the animals who *lived* in the shells.

Next Rachel turned her attention from the sea to the clouds. She wrote a television script called "Something About the Sky." The program was broadcast in March 1956. Then Rachel shifted her focus in yet another direction: viewing nature through a child's eyes.

Roger, her grandnephew, had been present in Rachel's life since he was a baby. Rachel's niece Marjorie brought Roger to the cottage in Maine summer after summer. Roger's father had died before Roger ever knew him, but in Rachel's house there were plenty of people to love a little boy.

Even before he could walk, Roger began to accompany Rachel on her ramblings. She wanted him to experience nature in all weathers, day and night. When Roger was a baby, Rachel had carried him down to the beach to meet the sea. The baby in her arms laughed with delight at the tumbling waters. As he grew older, Roger would sit on Rachel's lap, quietly watching the moon on the water.

Once, out walking in the woods near the house, Rachel pointed to a spruce tree seedling. She told Roger the tiny tree was a Christmas tree for squirrels, since it was just the right size. She described how the squirrels decorated their tree with shells and tiny pinecones.

They came to a smaller seedling. Keeping up the game, Rachel said the tinier tree was probably a Christmas tree for bugs. A larger tree became a Christmas tree for rabbits and woodchucks.

Enchanted with the idea of animals celebrating holidays, Roger would warn Rachel not to step on the Christmas trees.

Rachel wrote about their walks in an article that was published in *Woman's Home Companion* magazine. She realized the importance of sharing nature with a child, and she hoped parents would take their children on nature walks, too. The article was well received and several publishers urged Rachel to turn the article into a book. (Rachel always intended to do this, but never had the time. *The Sense of Wonder*—a book based on the article—was published a year after her death.)

Like the ebb and flow of the sea, the Carson household grew and shrank and grew again. Marjorie and Roger spent their summers at the Maine cottage. And there was always a cat. Now Jeffie the cat traveled from Maryland to Maine as a valued member of the family.

One moonlit night, Rachel and Marjorie went down to the beach to secure four-year-old Roger's raft, which was being pulled out to sea by the restless spring tides. The sand glittered with green and yellow specks, like emeralds and diamonds. Rachel and Marjorie scooped up handfuls of the sparkles. Then one of the sparkles flew away! It was a firefly, attracted by the shimmering sand. The firefly thought the sparkles were other fireflies. Rachel captured the hapless insect and put it in Roger's bucket to dry. Marjorie and Rachel giggled like schoolgirls over the incident.

In early 1957, Marjorie died of pneumonia. Rachel missed her very much. She had raised Marjorie like a daughter and had been close to her all her life. Like the firefly Rachel and Marjorie had watched that summer, a life had sparkled, then was gone.

Five-year-old Roger was left without any parents. Mrs. Carson was eighty-eight and in need of constant care. Nearing fifty, Rachel was not in good health herself. She was plagued with the arthritis that crippled so many members of her family, and she caught a lot of colds. But Rachel loved Roger as though he were her own son, so she adopted him.

So far Rachel's work had led her to the sea and even to the sky. Now she began to look around her and observe what was happening to the land. She did not like what she saw. Forests had been cut down, factories dumped their poisonous waste products into rivers, entire wildlands were cleared to make way for houses and roads. People were destroying the world.

Rachel had not been unaware of what was going on around her, even while she was so immersed in her studies of the sea. Shortly after World War II, in the mid-forties, Rachel and Shirley Briggs, a colleague at the Fish and Wildlife Service, had been assigned to put together a series of booklets called *Conservation in Action.* Inspired by material-gathering expeditions, Rachel often scribbled notes about the small creatures, such as spiders and crickets, that still fascinated her, just as they had when she was a child. She found herself listening to the crickets late one summer night. Had she ever really listened before?

Concentrating, she realized the cricket chorus was made up of individual voices. One cricket in particular had such a sweet, haunting voice, she named it the fairy bellringer. Rachel searched night after night for this cricket, but could never find it. The cricket remained hidden, sweetly chirping the message that summer was ending.

And now, more than ten years after listening to that cricket chorus, Rachel was afraid something else might be ending, too. The natural world was in grave danger, unless someone did something about it. Rachel was tired, but she had one more task before her.

Like the fairy bellringer, she would make herself heard. But she would not remain invisible.

(5)

Work That Has No End

Seven dead songbirds.

Rachel let the letter fall to her lap and closed her eyes. She had much to think about.

It was January 1958. The letter that distressed Rachel came from a friend, Olga Owens Huckins. Mrs. Huckins had witnessed a terrible sight. A plane had spewed a cloud of DDT over the small private bird sanctuary Mrs. Huckins owned. The pesticide was supposed to kill mosquitoes. The powerful chemical wiped out the mosquitoes all right, but it also killed other insects and many birds. Mrs. Huckins picked up seven dead birds around her home, heartsick over the needless deaths of innocent songbirds. Alarmed, she had written a letter to the *Boston Herald,* describing the incident and making a general plea to ban the spraying of pesticides from the air.

When her letter was published in the newspaper, Mrs. Huckins sent a copy to Rachel Carson. In her personal letter to Rachel, Mrs. Huckins urged Rachel to find someone in Washington who could help control these senseless mass sprayings.

Rachel knew what had to be done. She would write an article warning about the dangers of pesticides. No, she had tried that. Years before, after the war, Rachel had offered to write about the dangers of pesticides, but magazines had turned her down, even though she was a well-known author. She was told that advertisers, who buy space in magazines, would object to such a controversial piece. One manufacturer of canned baby food declared that an article such as Rachel proposed would cause panic among young mothers. People might stop buying their product. Companies weren't about to lose sales over a magazine article.

An article wouldn't adequately cover such a vast subject, anyway, Rachel felt. She would have to write a book.

She had planned to write a book about the earth, doing for the continents what she had done for the sea in *The Sea Around Us,* but that project would have to wait. Her friends tried to discourage her from writing about pesticides. Who would want to read about such a dreary topic?

Undaunted, Rachel began researching her subject. Pesticides are chemicals used to control insects and other pests. DDT (dichloro-diphenyl-trichloroethane) was the most popular pesticide. Widely used as a dust and a spray, DDT was touted as the "wonder" chemical. DDT saved time, money, and labor. Farmers, foresters, dairy people, and gardeners used a half billion pounds of the toxic substance per year. DDT declared war on insects. Crop-threatening insects lost— but so did harmless insects, birds, rabbits, squirrels, muskrats, even farm cats exposed to the chemical.

If DDT killed insects and small land animals, Rachel wondered, what was it doing to fish? She found out that the poisonous substance, which was washed by rainfall into creeks, also killed fish. Next she asked what effect DDT would have on humans if they ate vegetables and fruit sprayed with the deadly chemical. If people poisoned their food to protect it, weren't they poisoning themselves as well?

A dreary subject, indeed, but Rachel felt there would be no peace for her if she kept silent. It wasn't just the issue of seven dead birds. *All* life seemed to be threatened by human progress. But she would tackle the problem of pesticides first.

Rachel needed help to find answers. She sought the advice and opinions of experts. Biologists, naturalists, and other scientists sent her information from all over the world. She hired an assistant to help with typing and note-taking.

The book progressed slowly. Rachel sensed she would not have all the time in the world to write this book. Bouts of illness sometimes kept her bedridden for months. She gave up her bird walks and her hikes with Roger. All her energies were directed toward her work.

In December 1958, Mrs. Carson died, six months short of her ninetieth birthday. Not only did Rachel lose her mother, but she also lost her dearest friend. She remembered her mother's gentleness, the way she would put spiders out the door instead of killing them. She recalled how her mother encouraged her writing. Hearing her mother's voice in her memory, urging her on, Rachel worked harder than ever to complete her book.

She thought she would call the book "Man Against the Earth," but that didn't sound quite right. The title that was decided on came right from the book. In the first chapter, Rachel asks the reader why the birds have stopped singing, what has silenced the voices that are the sound of springtime? And so the book was titled *Silent Spring.*

Rachel mailed the completed manuscript to her publisher, never suspecting her book would change the course of history.

Silent Spring was scheduled to be published in September 1962. But that summer, before the book arrived in bookstores, parts appeared in the *New Yorker* magazine. The reaction to *Silent Spring* was anything but silent. According to a headline in the *New York Times,* Rachel Carson's book started a very noisy summer!

The chemical industry was up in arms. Here was a book that could put them out of business! Articles lashing out against *Silent Spring* attacked Rachel herself, saying she was a "nature nut." *Silent Spring* did not receive the consistently glowing attention in which Rachel's earlier books had basked. The reviews swung from harsh criticism to high praise. While some reviewers declared that the claims made in *Silent Spring* were false, others were glad to know about dangerous chemicals. Letters flooded Rachel's mailbox. Readers demanded something be done about pesticides.

The public clamored for Rachel to give speeches and grant interviews as before. This time, though, instead of simply autographing stacks of books, Rachel had to defend the conclusions she made in *Silent Spring.* She stood up against her accusers. People began to listen, and to recognize her achievement.

On January 7, 1963, Rachel was presented with the Schweitzer Medal of the Animal Welfare Institute. This award meant more to her than any of her previous awards or any that would come later. Rachel had dedicated *Silent Spring* to Albert Schweitzer, a man who had devoted his entire life to serving humankind. Albert Schweitzer had great respect and love for all forms of life. Rachel was proud to receive an award in his name.

Meanwhile, the storm over her book continued. The racket over *Silent Spring* was heard in the White House. President Kennedy set up a committee to study environmental hazards. Rachel met with the committee members in January 1963. The report, released the following May, agreed with Rachel's findings. As a result, hearings on pesticide control began in the Senate.

Again, Rachel went to Washington to testify. The Senate was packed with photographers, reporters, and television cameras. One senator remarked, upon meeting her, that *she* was the woman who had started the ruckus. He implied it was hard to believe such a small, quiet woman had caused such a commotion. But when Rachel presented her facts, people were convinced she knew what she was talking about.

Rachel spent the rest of the summer in Maine, enjoying the peacefulness of the sea. Here there were no television cameras pointing at her. There were no requests to give speeches. Lying on a blanket, Rachel watched the gulls wheeling in the sky. When the crickets began their end-of-summer song, Rachel and Roger went back to Maryland.

In the first week of December, Rachel traveled to New York to pick up three awards. The hue and cry over *Silent Spring* had died down. But even as she was being honored, Rachel would not let people forget the purpose of her book.

The National Audubon Society's medal represented rare praise—Rachel was the first woman ever to receive it. At the awards banquet, Rachel warned the guests that their work in conservation had no end. Next Rachel received a medal from the American Geographical Society for her contribution to the cause of conservation. Then Rachel was elected to the American Academy of Arts and Letters.

Throughout the writing and the defending of her book, Rachel battled ill health. She suffered a minor heart attack, her old enemy arthritis plagued her, and—most serious of all—she had cancer. Roger was now eleven. Rachel did not know how much longer she would be able to care for him. But as long as they had each other, she would make the most of every moment.

In the early spring of 1964, Rachel was cheered to hear the song of the first returning robin. Soon her yard would be filled with robins and thrashers, busily building nests and rearing young. Insects would hum in the rosebushes her brother was planting in her garden. The grass would teem with life.

After spring would come summer. A noisy, active, *lively* summer. Would she hear the crickets' song?

Rachel knew that she might not hear the crickets again. But she had accomplished much in her fifty-six years. She had done her best to preserve life. She had listened to the planet and let other people know what she had heard.

Even more important, she was part of the living, breathing, crawling, flying, walking, swimming, rooted thing called nature.

For now, that was enough.

59

Afterword

Rachel Louise Carson died of cancer on April 14, 1964. She left a legacy of memorable work, including bulletins, pamphlets, articles, essays, and books.

In 1980 Rachel was posthumously awarded the Presidential Medal of Freedom, the highest honor a civilian can achieve, by President Jimmy Carter. Her face graced a postage stamp in 1981.

Schools in Maryland and New York bear her name. Rachel's name also heads a wildlife refuge, a nature trail in Pennsylvania, and several research ships. Even a peregrine falcon was named after her.

Like her name, Rachel's work lives on. Though her books about the sea catapulted her to fame, it was *Silent Spring* that changed the way we view our environment. "Conservation" and "ecology" became household words.

Silent Spring brought results. DDT and other related chemicals have been almost completely banned in the United States, Canada, and other developed countries. Though dangerous pesticides are still being produced, other methods of managing crop pests are being promoted, such as the use of natural enemies (usually other insects) or biodegradable insecticides.

The Environmental Protection Agency (EPA) was formed to enforce controls on land use, factory waste, and many other hazards to our environment. The Clean Air Act and Clean Water Act were passed to curb pollution, while the Endangered Species Act protects our vanishing wildlife.

Silent Spring made us realize we have the power to stop damaging our planet and begin preserving our natural resources. But as Rachel cautioned fellow conservationists, it is work that has no end. We are also a part of the living, breathing, crawling, flying, walking, swimming, rooted thing called nature.

We must not forget it.

Books by Rachel Carson

Under the Sea-Wind. New York: Oxford University Press, 1952. (Originally published by Simon and Schuster, 1941.)

The Sea Around Us. New York: Oxford University Press, 1951.

The Edge of the Sea. Boston: Houghton Mifflin, 1955.

Silent Spring. Boston: Houghton Mifflin, 1962.

The Sense of Wonder. New York: Harper & Row, 1965.

Bibliography

Books:

Alexander, Taylor R., and George S. Fichter. *Ecology.* Racine, Wis.: Golden Press, 1973.

Brooks, Paul. *The House of Life: Rachel Carson at Work.* Boston: Houghton Mifflin, 1972.

Brooks, Paul. *Speaking for Nature: How Literary Naturalists from Henry Thoreau to Rachel Carson Have Shaped America.* Boston: Houghton Mifflin, 1980.

Carson, Rachel. *The Edge of the Sea.* Boston: Houghton Mifflin, 1955.

Carson, Rachel. *The Sense of Wonder.* New York: Harper & Row, 1965.

Carson, Rachel. *Silent Spring.* Boston: Houghton Mifflin, 1962.

Carson, Rachel. *Under the Sea-Wind.* New York: Oxford University Press, 1952.

Graham, Jr., Frank. *Since Silent Spring.* Boston: Houghton Mifflin, 1970.

Sterling, Philip. *Sea and Earth: The Life of Rachel Carson.* New York: Thomas Y. Crowell, 1970.

Stevens, Lawrence. *Ecology Basics.* Englewood Cliffs, N.J.: Prentice Hall, 1986.

Wayne, Bennet, ed. *They Loved the Land.* Champaign, Ill.: Garrard Publishing Co., 1974.

Other:

Briggs, Shirley. Interview with author. January 1991.

Carson, Rachel. Acceptance speech for John Burroughs Medal, 1952.

Carson, Rachel. Acceptance speech for National Book Award, 1952.

"The Gentle Storm Center." *Life* (1962): 105.